British Royal Family

From William the Conqueror to the Ho

GW01157583

Contents

The Normans 1066-1154

Who were They?

The Scandinavian Vikings - *raiders from the sea* - rejoicing in such wonderful names as Eystein the Noisy, Sweyn Forkbeard and Erik Bloodaxe, cut a huge swathe through Europe as far as Russia, and, in their state-of-the-art longships, even reached as far west as America. In England the ruling House of Wessex, **Alfred the Great**'s family, was plagued the most by the Danish Vikings and had to reach a compromise and allow them to settle in the area to the north and east of a line between London and Chester, the route of the old Roman Watling Street, which became known as *Danelaw*.

Meanwhile, other Danes led by **Rollo, a Norwegian Viking**, were granted lands in northern France by King Charles the Simple, who wanted to avoid further confrontation with them. One story says that when called upon to kiss the King's foot in homage, Rollo sent him flying as a reminder that he and his Vikings would always be a force to be reckoned with. Later Rollo converted to Christianity and changed his name to Robert.

Rollo's great-granddaughter, **Emma of Normandy**, married **Aethelred the Unready** of England, a man not cast in the same wise mould as his ancestor Alfred the Great, and who attacked the Danes living peacefully in Danelaw, with the result that Sweyn Forkbeard, King of Denmark, whose sister had been killed, arrived on the scene and forced him to flee abroad. In 1016, Sweyn's son **Canute** (Knut) became King of England – one of the most dedicated and competent the country has ever had. Aethelred died in exile and his widow packed off her children to her relations in Normandy and promptly married a much younger man – none other than King Canute himself!

When Canute died, a power struggle ensued between his sons, both of whom had very short reigns, and eventually Emma and Aethelred's exiled son, known because of his extreme piety as **Edward the Confessor**, emerged as the reluctant ruler.

Emma of Normandy's great-nephew, **Duke William of Normandy**, expected his kinsman King Edward to name him as his heir and so claimed the throne when the Confessor died; he also claimed to have had the promise of support from the country's leading nobleman, **Harold Godwinson**, **Earl of Wessex,** and was more than a little put out when it was Harold and not himself who was chosen by the Witan, a council of wise men. William defeated and killed Harold at Hastings in October 1066 and was crowned in Westminster Abbey on Christmas Day.

William the Conqueror was the son of Duke Robert (*the Devil*) and Arlette, a tanner's daughter – she later married one of the duke's followers and became the mother of **Odo**, **Bishop of Bayeux**, for whom the great Bayeux Tapestry was made.

The Conqueror's bachelor son **William II,** called **Rufus** because of his red complexion or red hair, was a powerful but unpopular ruler 'accidentally' killed in the New Forest; it was widely believed his brother Henry was party to the murder.

Henry I was a strong ruler in whose reign much was done to unite the Normans and the vanquished Saxons. His heir was drowned in the Channel, a disaster leading eventually to a terrible civil war between the cousins **Stephen and Matilda**. Matilda was defeated, but the death of Stephen's son meant the end of the Norman dynasty.

The Family of William the Conqueror,

Duke of Normandy and King of England.

(Although William's ancestor Rollo was a Norwegian Viking,
he led Danish raiders who settled in northern France)
The Normans ruled England from 1066 - 1154

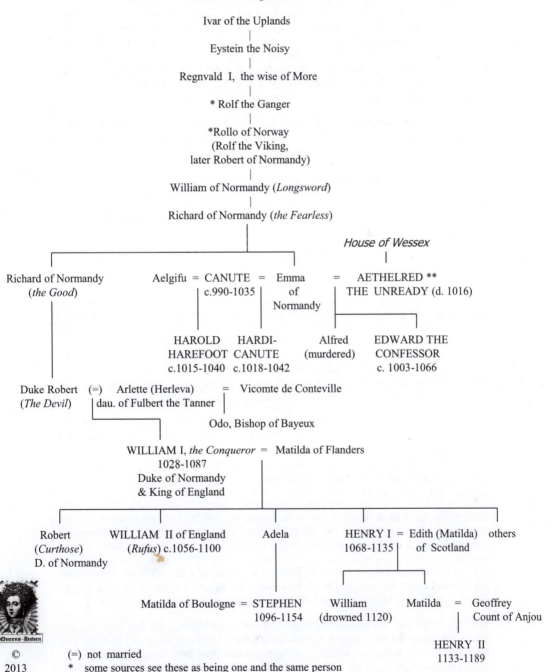

Ivar of the Uplands

Eystein the Noisy

Regnvald I, the wise of More

* Rolf the Ganger

*Rollo of Norway
(Rolf the Viking,
later Robert of Normandy)

William of Normandy (*Longsword*)

Richard of Normandy (*the Fearless*)

House of Wessex

Richard of Normandy (*the Good*)

Aelgifu = CANUTE = Emma of Normandy
c.990-1035

= AETHELRED ** THE UNREADY (d. 1016)

HAROLD HAREFOOT c.1015-1040

HARDI-CANUTE c.1018-1042

Alfred (murdered)

EDWARD THE CONFESSOR c. 1003-1066

Duke Robert (*The Devil*) (=) Arlette (Herleva) dau. of Fulbert the Tanner = Vicomte de Conteville

Odo, Bishop of Bayeux

WILLIAM I, *the Conqueror* 1028-1087 Duke of Normandy & King of England = Matilda of Flanders

Robert (*Curthose*) D. of Normandy

WILLIAM II of England (*Rufus*) c.1056-1100

Adela

HENRY I 1068-1135 = Edith (Matilda) of Scotland   others

Matilda of Boulogne = STEPHEN 1096-1154

William (drowned 1120)

Matilda = Geoffrey Count of Anjou

HENRY II 1133-1189

(=) not married
*   some sources see these as being one and the same person
** Edmund Ironside, Aethelred's son from his first
marriage, also died in 1016

2

The Plantagenets 1154-1399

Who were They?

They were the descendants of Henry I's daughter **Matilda** and **Geoffrey, Count of Anjou**. The Count took to wearing a sprig of broom or *planta genista* in his helmet, hence the name Plantagenet – which to us has a rather more romantic ring to it than plain old *broom* – although the name did not come into use until very much later.

Henry II inherited England and huge areas of France and further increased his power by marrying **Eleanor of Aquitaine**. Henry's most famous adversary was his one-time friend Thomas Becket, whom he made Archbishop of Canterbury, and who was murdered in his own cathedral in 1170. Queen Eleanor, partially motivated by anger at her husband's flagrant womanising, plotted against him with their sons and it was said that, even in death, he hated his son Richard so much that when the latter tried to pay his respects to his father's corpse the nose started to bleed.

Richard I himself was an itinerant adventurer who spent only 6 months of his 10-year reign in England, and only then to raise funds to fight the Crusades in the Holy Land. His brother **King John** is best remembered for signing Magna Carta, losing his treasure and crown jewels in The Wash and losing the French territories, including Normandy itself.

The reign of the not very pleasant **Henry III** saw the beginnings of democracy, but the efforts of his brother-in-law, Simon de Montfort, to include commoners in decision-making ended in disaster, with Simon hacked to pieces on the battlefield.

Edward I, who has the epitaph *Hammer of the Scots* on his tomb, had the Scots rebel Sir William Wallace hanged, drawn and quartered at Smithfield, outside St Bartholomew's (Bart's) Hospital. Edward and **Eleanor of Castile** were married for 36 years; devastated by her death he had the Eleanor Crosses erected at each place the cortège stopped on its journey between Lincoln and London. Nine years later, at the age of 60, he married a 17-year-old French princess and fathered three more children.

Edward II was the elder surviving son of Edward I. As a child he was isolated, afraid and lonely and found what few friends he had amongst the servants. He married and had children but he was easily influenced by his male favourites, and was deposed by his wife and her lover – gory tradition has it that he was killed by having a red hot poker pushed into his bowel.

Edward III was more like his grandfather than his effeminate father and decided that, since his mother was of the royal house of France, he had a claim to that country's throne: thus began the Hundred Years' War. These were also the years of the terrible Black Death, which claimed over a third of the population. Edward had an eye for the ladies and founded the Most Noble Order of the Garter when the Fair Maid of Kent's garter fell down at a party – it was a bit of a talking point, then, when she later married his son and heir, **Edward, the Black Prince**, a famous soldier who supported the House of Commons in its struggle against royal corruption.

The Black Prince, weakened by the dysentery contracted on his last military campaign, died the year before his father, so the prince's 10-year-old son became **Richard II**; he became increasingly mentally unstable and was deposed by his cousin **Henry Bolingbroke**, son of **John of Gaunt**, and murdered at the age of 33.

The Plantagenets 1154 – 1399

His [red] hair is not in fear of the losses of baldness... his leonine face is rather square. Peter of Blois on Henry II, 1177

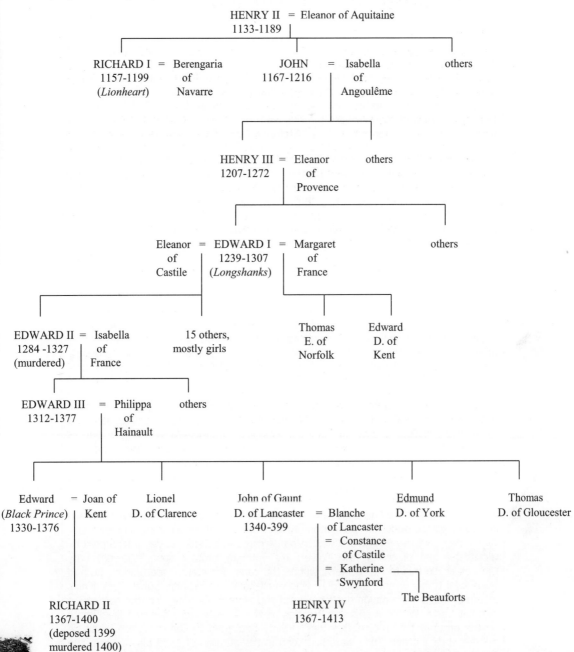

HENRY II = Eleanor of Aquitaine
1133-1189

RICHARD I = Berengaria
1157-1199   of
(*Lionheart*)   Navarre

JOHN = Isabella
1167-1216   of
Angoulême

others

HENRY III = Eleanor
1207-1272   of
Provence

others

Eleanor = EDWARD I = Margaret
of   1239-1307   of
Castile (*Longshanks*) France

others

EDWARD II = Isabella
1284 -1327   of
(murdered)   France

15 others,
mostly girls

Thomas
E. of
Norfolk

Edward
D. of
Kent

EDWARD III = Philippa
1312-1377   of
Hainault

others

Edward   – Joan of
(*Black Prince*) Kent
1330-1376

Lionel
D. of Clarence

John of Gaunt
D. of Lancaster
1340-399

= Blanche
of Lancaster
= Constance
of Castile
= Katherine
Swynford

Edmund
D. of York

Thomas
D. of Gloucester

RICHARD II
1367-1400
(deposed 1399
murdered 1400)

HENRY IV
1367-1413

The Beauforts

...he was being carried to burial clothed in royal robes, wearing a crown of gold upon his head and gold shoes and spurs on his feet, girded with sword, face uncovered...his son Count Richard came to meet him...and blood at once began to flow from the nostrils of the dead king, as if his spirit was indignant at Richard's arrival.
Chronicle of Benedict of Peterborough, 1189 – the funeral of Henry II

The Houses of Lancaster and York 1399–1485

Who were They?

The Lancastrians were descended from Edward III's son **John of Gaunt**, **Duke of Lancaster**, through two of his three separate families from three marriages, while the forebears of the Yorkists were Gaunt's brothers **Lionel, Duke of Clarence**, and **Edmund, Duke of York**, whose families were eventually united by the marriage of **Anne Mortimer** (Clarence branch) to **Richard, Earl of Cambridge** (York branch).

The Clarences were the expected heirs of the childless Richard II but it was **Henry Bolingbroke of Lancaster** who usurped the throne. (*Duke of Lancaster* has been one of the monarch's titles ever since – Queen Elizabeth II is the present duke.) Bolingbroke, as **Henry IV**, had a terribly difficult and guilt-ridden reign and died worn out in his mid-40's. His son, the hero **Henry V**, died young, of dysentery – the scourge of the medieval armies – and the inevitable conflict between the rival branches of the Plantagenet family reached its peak in the reign of his son.

Henry VI was a baby when his father died and as he grew up he was of the opposite disposition to Henry V, being a gentle and uninspiring soul quite unsuited for the position of charismatic late medieval monarch. His French wife, **Margaret of Anjou**, was another matter altogether and her arrogance, favouritism and meddling in politics, coupled with Henry's ineptitude, resulted in the Wars of the Roses. **Richard of York**, the son of Anne Mortimer and Richard of Cambridge, was called upon to act as regent for Henry VI during his bouts of mental illness and a possible way forward was to make him his heir; the powerful Queen Margaret would have none of it, and when hostilities broke out even led an army against Richard herself.

Margaret of Anjou caught up with Richard of York and executed him after the Battle of Wakefield in 1460 and his head, with that of his son Edmund, was displayed on a spike on the walls of the city of York. His youngest son, Richard, was only 8, but his 18-year-old heir, the Earl of March, deposed Henry VI and became **Edward IV**. The struggles continued for many years culminating in the murder of Henry VI in the Tower of London; Queen Margaret was eventually sent back to France and died in poverty.

Edward IV died at the age of 40 and had left instructions for his 12-year-old son and heir to be placed under the protection of Richard, Duke of Gloucester until crowned. When the new **King Edward V** was being escorted to London he was intercepted by Gloucester and placed in the Tower; his younger brother soon followed. Why Gloucester did this to his nephews will be the cause for eternal speculation: he had been loyal to his brother Edward IV who must have trusted him, but the boy king's maternal family were dangerously powerful and were proceeding with the coronation in great haste. Within weeks the **Princes in the Tower** were declared illegitimate on the grounds that their father was already betrothed to someone else when he married their mother. They were last seen in the autumn of 1483 playing near the Garden Tower, thereafter named the 'Bloody Tower', since it is thought they could have been murdered there.

The Duke of Gloucester became **Richard III**, but in less than two years he was dead, killed at the Battle of Bosworth in 1485, his crown going to the victor, the virtually unknown Welsh Lancastrian, **Henry Tudor, Earl of Richmond**.

The Houses of Lancaster and York 1399-1485

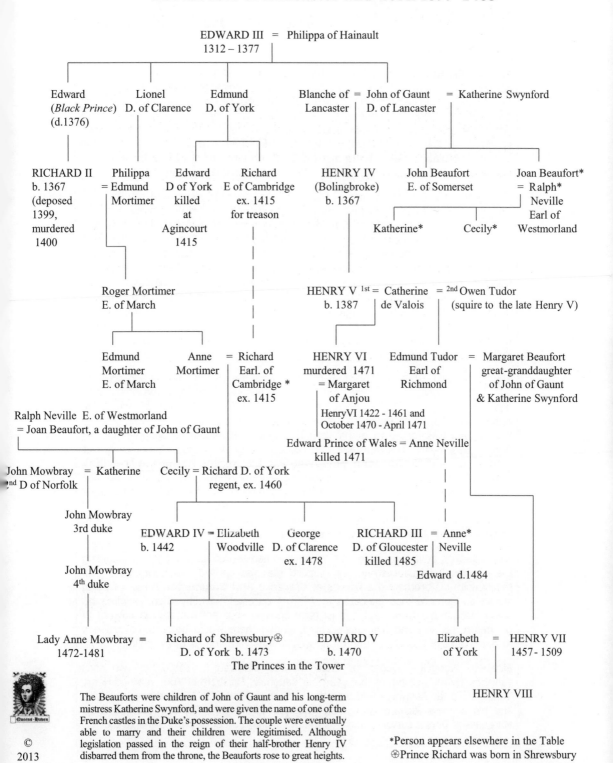

EDWARD III = Philippa of Hainault
1312 – 1377

Edward (*Black Prince*) (d.1376)

Lionel D. of Clarence

Edmund D. of York

Blanche of Lancaster = John of Gaunt D. of Lancaster = Katherine Swynford

RICHARD II b. 1367 (deposed 1399, murdered 1400)

Philippa = Edmund Mortimer

Edward D of York killed at Agincourt 1415

Richard E of Cambridge ex. 1415 for treason

HENRY IV (Bolingbroke) b. 1367

John Beaufort E. of Somerset

Joan Beaufort* = Ralph* Neville Earl of Westmorland

Katherine* Cecily*

Roger Mortimer E. of March

HENRY V 1st = Catherine de Valois = 2nd Owen Tudor (squire to the late Henry V) b. 1387

Edmund Mortimer E. of March

Anne Mortimer = Richard Earl. of Cambridge * ex. 1415

HENRY VI murdered 1471 = Margaret of Anjou

HenryVI 1422 - 1461 and October 1470 - April 1471

Edmund Tudor Earl of Richmond = Margaret Beaufort great-granddaughter of John of Gaunt & Katherine Swynford

Ralph Neville E. of Westmorland = Joan Beaufort, a daughter of John of Gaunt

Edward Prince of Wales = Anne Neville killed 1471

John Mowbray 2nd D of Norfolk = Katherine

Cecily = Richard D. of York regent, ex. 1460

John Mowbray 3rd duke

EDWARD IV b. 1442 = Elizabeth Woodville

George D. of Clarence ex. 1478

RICHARD III D. of Gloucester killed 1485 = Anne* Neville

Edward d.1484

John Mowbray 4th duke

Lady Anne Mowbray = 1472-1481

Richard of Shrewsbury⊛ D. of York b. 1473

EDWARD V b. 1470

The Princes in the Tower

Elizabeth of York = HENRY VII 1457- 1509

HENRY VIII

The Beauforts were children of John of Gaunt and his long-term mistress Katherine Swynford, and were given the name of one of the French castles in the Duke's possession. The couple were eventually able to marry and their children were legitimised. Although legislation passed in the reign of their half-brother Henry IV disbarred them from the throne, the Beauforts rose to great heights.

*Person appears elsewhere in the Table
⊛Prince Richard was born in Shrewsbury

The Woodvilles – a shock to the Medieval System

Who were they?

The first **Sir Richard Woodville** fought for Henry V and received lands in France. His son, Sir Richard (II) was born around 1405 and knighted in 1426. This younger Sir Richard caused bad feeling by marrying **Jacquetta St Pol** of Luxembourg, for not only was she young and very attractive, she was also very rich, being the widow of Henry V's brother, the Duke of Bedford, and way beyond the humble Woodville's sphere. They had 14 children, the oldest being Elizabeth born in 1437. At about the age of 15 **Elizabeth Woodville** married **Sir John Grey of Groby,** with whom she had two sons, **Thomas Grey,** born in 1455 and **Richard Grey**, born 1458.

Originally in the Lancastrian camp, the Woodvilles changed sides after the Battle of Towton in 1461. In 1463 Elizabeth petitioned the young Edward IV for help in sorting out her late husband's assets. The smitten King wanted her to be his mistress but she refused and he married her in secret the following year. The new Queen's large family, aided and abetted by King Edward, saw a meteoric rise in their fortunes, much to the anger of the established nobility who regarded them as dangerous upstarts. Her father was created Earl Rivers and appointed Lord Treasurer in 1466 and Constable of England in 1467. **Richard Neville, Earl of Warwick** had helped put Edward IV on the throne, but now saw his position eclipsed by the newcomers. He had been trying to secure an alliance with a foreign princess and was humiliated to find his young master was already secretly married. Neville eventually defected to the Lancastrians and restored Henry VI, hence the name 'Warwick the Kingmaker'.

Thanks to her husband's conniving, not only were the Queen's father and brothers advanced to positions of power and influence, her sisters made some of the best possible arranged matches. Naturally, this caused further friction among noble fathers who felt they had been robbed, especially when the heir to the Duke of Buckingham was forced to marry Katherine Woodville, whom he despised for her humble beginnings. The marriage that caused the greatest disgust, however, was between 19-year-old **Sir John Woodville** and the wealthy **Katherine (Neville)**, 67-year-old widow of John Mowbray, second Duke of Norfolk, described at the time as 'a diabolical marriage' and putting him in control of her fortune. The Dowager was an aunt of 'the Kingmaker' and perhaps it is not surprising that Earl Rivers and his son John, then still only in his early twenties, were captured by Lancastrians at Chepstow in 1469 and beheaded at Kenilworth.

King Edward's advancement of the Woodvilles had the effect not only of alienating the nobility, both Lancastrian and Yorkist, but also caused a rift within his own family, with his brothers the **Dukes of Clarence and Gloucester** in fear of being sidelined. Clarence was executed in 1478. Gloucester was, by then, building his power base in the North and it must have become apparent that should Edward IV die before his son and heir gained his majority, there would be a tussle between Richard, Duke of Gloucester and the Woodville family for control of the child.

Elizabeth Woodville, Queen of England, was widowed in 1483, her two sons vanishing by the autumn of that year; her daughter, Elizabeth of York, married Henry Tudor, victor at Bosworth and was the mother of **Henry VIII**. Anthony Woodville and his nephew Richard Grey were executed by Richard III, but Thomas Grey, Marquess of Dorset survived and was the great-grandfather of **Lady Jane Grey**.

The Woodvilles

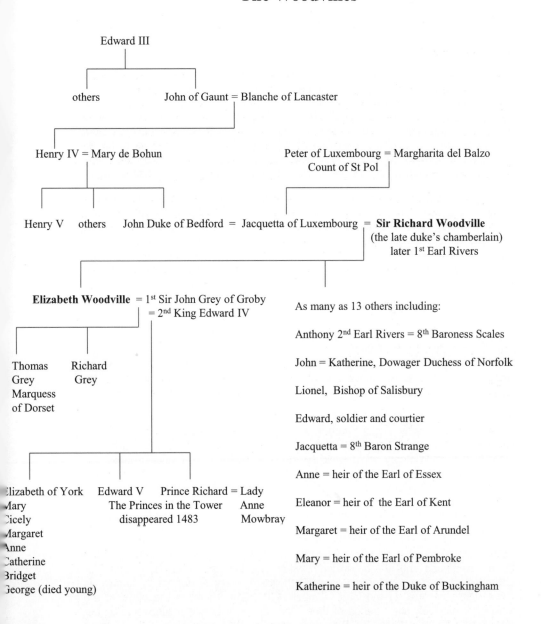

Edward III

others — John of Gaunt = Blanche of Lancaster

Henry IV = Mary de Bohun

Peter of Luxembourg = Margharita del Balzo
Count of St Pol

Henry V   others   John Duke of Bedford = Jacquetta of Luxembourg = **Sir Richard Woodville**
(the late duke's chamberlain)
later 1st Earl Rivers

Elizabeth Woodville = 1st Sir John Grey of Groby
= 2nd King Edward IV

Thomas
Grey
Marquess
of Dorset

Richard
Grey

Elizabeth of York
Mary
Cicely
Margaret
Anne
Catherine
Bridget
George (died young)

Edward V   Prince Richard = Lady
The Princes in the Tower   Anne
disappeared 1483   Mowbray

As many as 13 others including:

Anthony 2nd Earl Rivers = 8th Baroness Scales

John = Katherine, Dowager Duchess of Norfolk

Lionel, Bishop of Salisbury

Edward, soldier and courtier

Jacquetta = 8th Baron Strange

Anne = heir of the Earl of Essex

Eleanor = heir of the Earl of Kent

Margaret = heir of the Earl of Arundel

Mary = heir of the Earl of Pembroke

Katherine = heir of the Duke of Buckingham

On Thursday the fifteenth day of the month she came out of the Queen's chamber at Westminster and so proceeded through the King's great chamber and into the White Hall, and so proceeded into St Stephen's chamber, being attended by great estates and many ladies and gentlewomen, my Lord the noble Count of Lincoln led her on the right hand and upon the second hand the noble Count Rivers.

An account by an anonymous observer at the marriage in January 1478 of the younger son of Elizabeth Woodville and King Edward IV, who was aged four, to the Dowager Duchess of Norfolk's great-granddaughter, Lady Anne Mowbray, aged five, the last of her illustrious line, whose fortune Edward IV appropriated for his son. The noble 'Count' Rivers is Anthony Woodville.

The Tudors 1485-1603

Who were they?

The Tudors were a relatively obscure Welsh family from Anglesey. Henry V died young and his widow, Queen Catherine de Valois, retired to Leeds Castle in Kent and later secretly married her late husband's squire, **Owen Tudor**, bearing him several children before their secret was discovered. When the truth came out Catherine withdrew in disgrace to a nunnery in Bermondsey and Owen was jailed but escaped, only to become a casualty of the Wars of the Roses. The Yorkists beheaded him in Hereford market place where a mad woman washed the blood from his severed head and combed the matted hair. Docile Henry VI bore no ill will toward his half-siblings.

Owen's son, **Edmund Tudor**, married **Lady Margaret Beaufort**, a descendant of Edward III's son John of Gaunt and his third wife Katherine Swynford. Lady Margaret's only child was **Henry Tudor**, born when she was only 13 and recently widowed for the second time; Henry became the leader of the Lancastrians and defeated the Yorkist Richard III at the Battle of Bosworth in 1485. Henry Tudor's claim to the throne was very weak – especially since the original Beauforts had been barred from the line of succession by their half-brother Henry IV.

Henry Tudor, as **Henry VII**, proved to be the steadying influence and firm ruler needed to bring the Wars of the Roses to its conclusion. In order to help heal the murderous rift between the royal factions he married the head of the house of York, the beautiful **Elizabeth of York**, sister of the Princes in the Tower. Their eldest son and heir, Arthur, Prince of Wales, married the Spanish princess **Catherine of Aragon** but died a few months later. Henry VII then made arrangements for Catherine to be betrothed to his surviving son and new heir, Prince Henry.

Henry VIII became king at 17 and was very popular, presenting a sharp contrast to his serious and penny-pinching father. Affairs of state were put into the hands of capable people, notably Cardinal Wolsey, the son of an Ipswich butcher, but when he wanted something Henry could wield his royal authority with a vindictiveness and ferocity too terrible to contemplate – as Wolsey would discover. Tired of the Pope's authority in his kingdom, and irked because the Roman Catholic Church refused to allow him to divorce Catherine of Aragon, Henry set himself up as Head of the Church in England and duly confiscated the lands and properties owned by the monasteries.

Edward VI succeeded his father when he was only 9 years old, and reform of the Church continued until the boy's death, when his half-sister **Mary I**, daughter of Catherine of Aragon, restored Roman Catholicism. Mary is universally known as *Bloody Mary* because of the large number of Reformist heretics she burnt at the stake in a relatively short period of time. Her unpopularity was made worse by her marriage to Philip of Spain. The Reformist attempt at the beginning of the reign to put **Lady Jane Grey** on the throne resulted in the tragedy of her execution at the age of 17.

Elizabeth I, Anne Boleyn's daughter, was a colourful and attractive academic genius blessed with good advisors, good health and a large amount of common sense; she could also be unreasonable, indecisive and unfairly penny-pinching. In her reign the Church of England was fully established. Elizabeth lived her whole life under the spectre of assassination, but nevertheless she was a great and long-lived queen.

The Tudors 1485 – 1603

We all hungered after a prince so long that there was as much rejoicing as at the birth of John the Baptist.
Bishop Hugh Latimer on the birth of Prince Edward in 1537. Latimer was burnt at the stake by Mary I in 1555

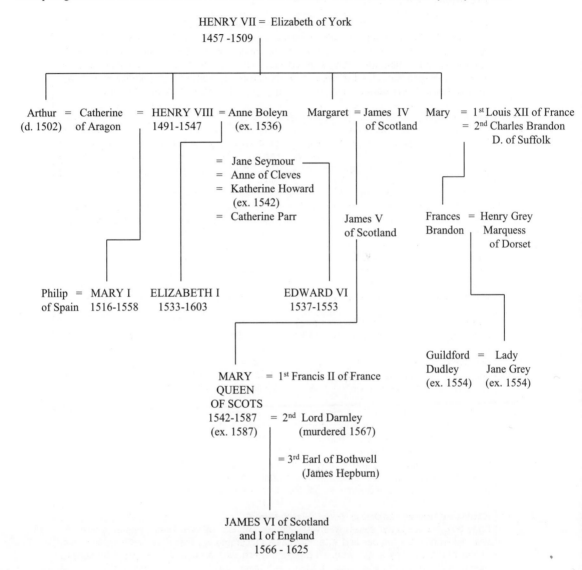

HENRY VII = Elizabeth of York
1457 -1509

Arthur = Catherine = HENRY VIII = Anne Boleyn   Margaret = James IV   Mary = 1ˢᵗ Louis XII of France
(d. 1502)   of Aragon   1491-1547   (ex. 1536)   of Scotland   = 2ⁿᵈ Charles Brandon
                                                                                          D. of Suffolk

= Jane Seymour
= Anne of Cleves
= Katherine Howard
  (ex. 1542)   James V   Frances = Henry Grey
= Catherine Parr   of Scotland   Brandon   Marquess
                                                                 of Dorset

Philip = MARY I   ELIZABETH I   EDWARD VI
of Spain 1516-1558 1533-1603   1537-1553

                                                          Guildford = Lady
                                                          Dudley   Jane Grey
MARY = 1ˢᵗ Francis II of France   (ex. 1554)   (ex. 1554)
QUEEN
OF SCOTS
1542-1587 = 2ⁿᵈ Lord Darnley
(ex. 1587)   (murdered 1567)

          = 3ʳᵈ Earl of Bothwell
            (James Hepburn)

JAMES VI of Scotland
and I of England
1566 - 1625

ex. executed

You have in various ways and manners attempted to take my life and to bring my kingdom to destruction
by bloodshed. These treasons will be proved to you and made manifest.
Letter from Queen Elizabeth I to Mary Queen of Scots at the start of her trial, October 1586.

Remember that the theatre of the world is wider than the realm of England.
Mary's warning to her judges, October 1586

©
2013

Henry VIII and His Wives

Catherine of Aragon (*married 1509-33 – **divorced***)
With no legitimate male heir after nearly 20 years of marriage – and a roving eye – King Henry VIII petitioned the Pope for a divorce from Catherine of Aragon, on the grounds that she had first been his brother's wife. The Pope would not oblige and over a period of nearly 9 years Henry and his new love, Anne Boleyn, made life dangerous and unbearable for Catherine and her daughter, Mary, who was deprived of her place in the succession. In order to get his divorce Henry had to break with the Church of Rome and found his own Church with himself as the Head. Catherine died of cancer in 1536; Henry had married Anne in 1533.

Anne Boleyn (*married 1533-36 – **beheaded***)
Anne was a maid-of-honour to Queen Catherine when the King first fell for her beguiling French manners, a result of her training at the French Court, and her beautiful dark eyes. Her sister had already been his mistress but Anne withheld her own favours until he was sure to make her his queen – a process that took 6 years. His infatuation with her was legendary and her hold over him incredibly powerful. She was an intelligent woman who drew Henry's attention to the book that gave him the idea of being total master of his realm, for which he would have to end the power of the Pope in England; it also led to her becoming his queen. Anne's treatment of Queen Catherine and her daughter bordered on the despicable, yet one cannot help but feel uneasy at the brutal and unjust nature of her own downfall. Once Anne was his wife, Henry was soon bored, even before their daughter Elizabeth was born in 1533. Miscarriages and stillbirths followed, and Anne was fighting a losing battle after she miscarried of a male child shortly after Catherine of Aragon died. In the spring of 1536 she was charged with multiple adultery with courtiers, including her own brother, beheaded, and buried under the floor of St Peter ad Vincula, the prisoners' church within the Tower.

Jane Seymour (*married 1536-37 – **died***)
Anne was beheaded on 19th May 1536 and Jane Seymour was betrothed to Henry the next day and they were married by the end of the month. By now the little Princess Elizabeth had been deprived of her title and rights to succeed and Jane did what she could to make life easier for her and for her long-suffering half-sister Mary. The domestic harmony ended abruptly the next year with Queen Jane's death following the birth of her son, Prince Edward.

Anne of Cleves (*married for 6 months in 1540 – **divorced***)
There was no enthusiastic queue forming to become Henry's fourth wife! Eventually he agreed with his chief minister Thomas Cromwell that a German Protestant princess would be an excellent choice. However, she was nothing like Hans Holbein's lovely portrait, and her lack of refinement disgusted Henry, who, true to form, was already looking elsewhere; Cromwell was executed. Anne was no fool, though: she liked England and her new prosperity and agreed to a lucrative divorce, so gaining Henry's friendship for the rest of his life.

Katherine Howard (*married 1540-42 – **beheaded***)
Anne Boleyn's teenaged cousin was wife number five, but by now Henry was an obese 50-year-old with a foul temper and a terribly painful ulcerated leg that oozed evil-smelling pus. Young Katherine was a girl with a racy past which was brought to Henry's attention 16 months after their marriage. This, and her more recent involvement with his trusted servant Thomas Culpeper, resulted in Katherine being beheaded in the Tower at the age of about 21.

Catherine Parr (*married 1543-47 – **survived***)
Henry VIII was 32-year-old Catherine Parr's third husband but she had been hoping to marry Thomas Seymour, Jane's brother. She was very intelligent and was a capable regent during Henry's absence abroad. She was also a kind stepmother to his children and was instrumental in the two girls being reinstated in the line of succession. Within weeks of the King's death she married 40-year-old Seymour but was devastated when he started pursuing her step-daughter, the 14-year-old Princess Elizabeth, whose guardians the couple were, and who lived with them. Catherine died only months afterwards, following the birth of her only child.

The Descent of Henry VIII and his Wives from King Edward I

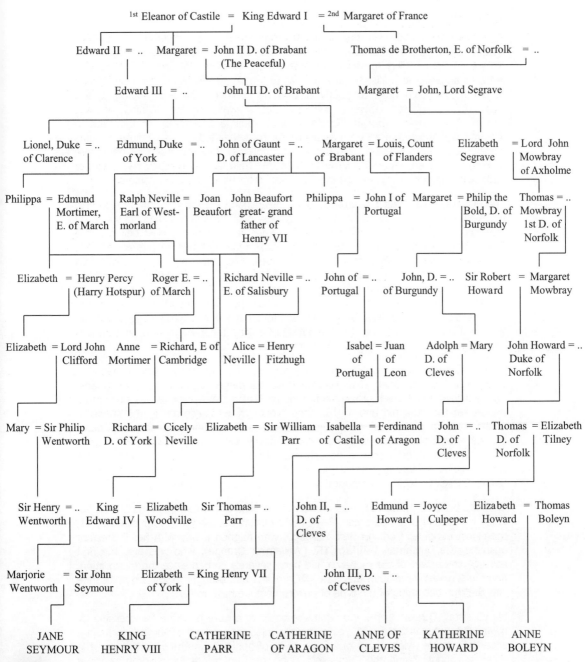

¹ˢᵗ Eleanor of Castile = King Edward I = ²ⁿᵈ Margaret of France

Edward II = .. Margaret = John II D. of Brabant (The Peaceful)

Thomas de Brotherton, E. of Norfolk = ..

Edward III = .. John III D. of Brabant

Margaret = John, Lord Segrave

Lionel, Duke of Clarence = .. | Edmund, Duke of York = .. | John of Gaunt D. of Lancaster = .. | Margaret of Brabant = Louis, Count of Flanders | Elizabeth Segrave = Lord John Mowbray of Axholme

Philippa = Edmund Mortimer, E. of March | Ralph Neville = Joan Beaufort, Earl of Westmorland | John Beaufort great-grand father of Henry VII | Philippa = John I of Portugal | Margaret = Philip the Bold, D. of Burgundy | Thomas = .. Mowbray 1st D. of Norfolk

Elizabeth = Henry Percy (Harry Hotspur) | Roger E. = .. of March | Richard Neville = .. E. of Salisbury | John of = .. Portugal | John, D. = .. of Burgundy | Sir Robert = Margaret Howard Mowbray

Elizabeth = Lord John Clifford | Anne = Richard, E of Mortimer Cambridge | Alice = Henry Neville Fitzhugh | Isabel = Juan of of Portugal Leon | Adolph = Mary D. of Cleves | John Howard = .. Duke of Norfolk

Mary = Sir Philip Wentworth | Richard = Cicely D. of York Neville | Elizabeth = Sir William Parr | Isabella = Ferdinand of Castile of Aragon | John = .. D. of Cleves | Thomas = Elizabeth D. of Tilney Norfolk

Sir Henry = .. Wentworth | King = Elizabeth Edward IV Woodville | Sir Thomas = .. Parr | John II, = .. D. of Cleves | Edmund = Joyce Howard Culpeper | Elizabeth = Thomas Howard Boleyn

Marjorie = Sir John Wentworth Seymour | Elizabeth = King Henry VII of York | John III, D. = .. of Cleves

JANE SEYMOUR | **KING HENRY VIII** | **CATHERINE PARR** | **CATHERINE OF ARAGON** | **ANNE OF CLEVES** | **KATHERINE HOWARD** | **ANNE BOLEYN**

Queens-Haven

...[she is] not one of the handsomest women in the world; she is of middling stature, swarthy complexion, long neck, wide mouth, bosom not much raised, [but] eyes which are black and beautiful.
A Venetian diplomat who saw Anne Boleyn in 1532

© 2013

The Stuarts 1603-1714

Who Were They?

They were descended from the Hereditary High Stewards of Scotland. When **Mary Queen of Scots**, a great-grandchild of Henry VII of England, was deposed, her baby son became **King James VI** of Scotland and was brought up in the Protestant faith. As an adult he realised that if he was to inherit the English crown from Queen Elizabeth he would have to subtly disown his mother, who was hoping to see Elizabeth assassinated, thereby showing that it was not for nothing he was known as *the wisest fool in Christendom*. He built a fine tomb for Elizabeth in Westminster Abbey and an even finer one for his beheaded mother, whose remains were brought from Peterborough Cathedral. English Catholics hoped that once here as King of England, James I & VI would reinstate their faith – the Gunpowder Plot of 1605 was an amateurish attempt at assassination for his tardiness in doing so.

The diminutive **Charles I** has the dubious distinction of being our only monarch to be executed – the traditional method of disposing of superfluous monarchs was by murdering them. His downfall was due in large measure to his rigid belief in the Divine Right of Kings, which meant that as God's representative he was answerable to nobody – especially Parliament. People marvelled that such a good man, who was a model father and husband, could be so bad at being a king; his French Catholic wife Henrietta Maria's influence upon his judgement was also greatly resented.
Whether Charles I deserved to die will always be a bone of contention. It was a cold winter's day when he was led to the scaffold outside the Banqueting House in Whitehall and he had taken the precaution of asking for a warm shirt to stop him shivering, lest the onlookers thought he trembled with fear.

Oliver Cromwell, a commoner, emerged as the country's leader amid the disastrous Civil War from 1642-49 with Royalists ranged against Parliamentarians, and families fighting each other. Many thought that the new regime was even more oppressive than the old and in 1660 the monarchy was restored in the shape of **Charles II**, a 6-foot-tall, good-living, overdressed libertine who fathered many children – unfortunately none to his wife. Cromwell had died in 1658 and was buried in Westminster Abbey, only to be exhumed, beheaded and hung in chains at the great gallows at Tyburn (present day Marble Arch). In 1960 his head was buried at Sidney Sussex College in Cambridge, where he had been a student.

Charles's brother, **James II**, was unpopular because of his Catholic sympathies, so, when his second wife had a son, James was quickly deposed in favour of **Mary II**, the eldest daughter from his first marriage, who reigned jointly with her Protestant husband, the Dutchman **William III** (William of Orange), who was also her first cousin. The power of the monarch had been severely curbed since the Restoration, and the Glorious Revolution that saw off James II and brought in William of Orange was the true beginning of the type of government we have today.

Mary's sister, **Queen Anne**, did what she could to ensure the Stuart succession by having 18 pregnancies in 16 years, mainly miscarriages and stillbirths, including, apparently, male twins where one foetus was of about 3 months gestation and the other of about 7 months. However, none of Queen Anne's children reached adolescence and a new monarch would have to be found from overseas.

The Stuarts 1603 – 1714

I have tried him drunk and I have tried him sober and there is nothing in him!
Charles II's views on Prince George of Denmark, husband of his niece, the future Queen Anne

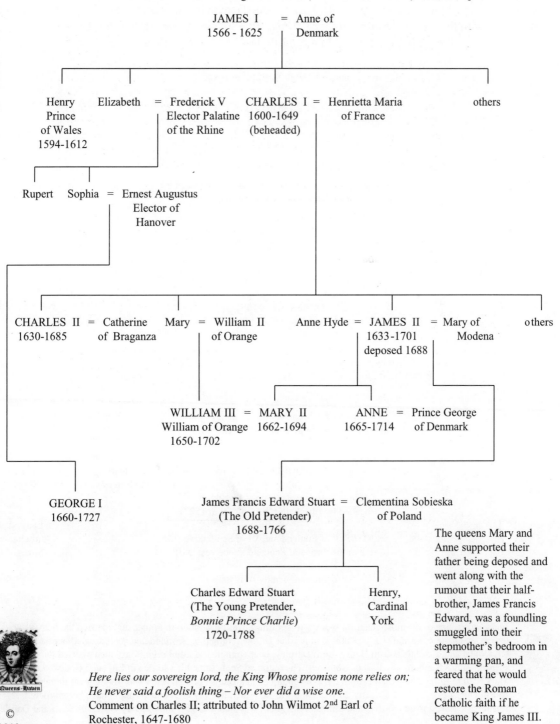

JAMES I = Anne of
1566 - 1625   Denmark

Henry | Elizabeth = Frederick V | CHARLES I = Henrietta Maria | others
Prince | Elector Palatine | 1600-1649 | of France
of Wales | of the Rhine | (beheaded)
1594-1612

Rupert | Sophia = Ernest Augustus
Elector of
Hanover

CHARLES II = Catherine | Mary = William II | Anne Hyde = JAMES II = Mary of | others
1630-1685 | of Braganza | of Orange | 1633-1701 | Modena
deposed 1688

WILLIAM III = MARY II | ANNE = Prince George
William of Orange | 1662-1694 | 1665-1714 | of Denmark
1650-1702

GEORGE I | James Francis Edward Stuart = Clementina Sobieska
1660-1727 | (The Old Pretender) | of Poland
1688-1766

Charles Edward Stuart | Henry,
(The Young Pretender, | Cardinal
Bonnie Prince Charlie) | York
1720-1788

The queens Mary and Anne supported their father being deposed and went along with the rumour that their half-brother, James Francis Edward, was a foundling smuggled into their stepmother's bedroom in a warming pan, and feared that he would restore the Roman Catholic faith if he became King James III.

Here lies our sovereign lord, the King Whose promise none relies on;
He never said a foolish thing – Nor ever did a wise one.
Comment on Charles II; attributed to John Wilmot 2nd Earl of
Rochester, 1647-1680

The Stuart Ancestors of Mary, Queen of Scots

The Stuarts, or Stewards, were originally named Fitzalan and came from England; they adopted the name Stewart when they became Hereditary Stewards of Scotland. Through their connections with the French royal family they changed the spelling to Stuart, which was easier for the French to pronounce. As a dynasty they had a very difficult time.

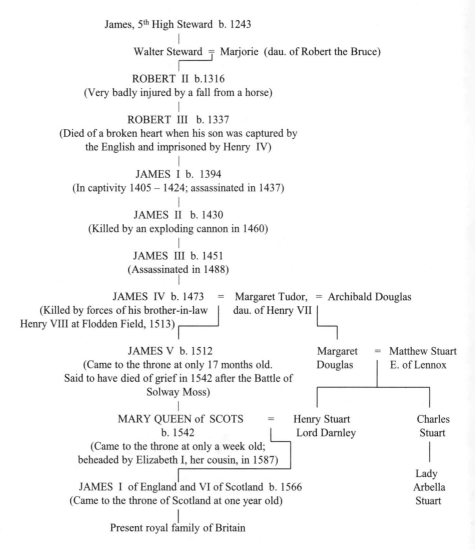

James, 5ᵗʰ High Steward b. 1243

Walter Steward = Marjorie (dau. of Robert the Bruce)

ROBERT II b.1316
(Very badly injured by a fall from a horse)

ROBERT III b. 1337
(Died of a broken heart when his son was captured by
the English and imprisoned by Henry IV)

JAMES I b. 1394
(In captivity 1405 – 1424; assassinated in 1437)

JAMES II b. 1430
(Killed by an exploding cannon in 1460)

JAMES III b. 1451
(Assassinated in 1488)

JAMES IV b. 1473   = Margaret Tudor, = Archibald Douglas
(Killed by forces of his brother-in-law   dau. of Henry VII
Henry VIII at Flodden Field, 1513)

JAMES V b. 1512   Margaret   = Matthew Stuart
(Came to the throne at only 17 months old.   Douglas   E. of Lennox
Said to have died of grief in 1542 after the Battle of
Solway Moss)

MARY QUEEN of SCOTS   = Henry Stuart   Charles
b. 1542   Lord Darnley   Stuart
(Came to the throne at only a week old;
beheaded by Elizabeth I, her cousin, in 1587)

Lady
Arbella
JAMES I of England and VI of Scotland b. 1566   Stuart
(Came to the throne of Scotland at one year old)

Present royal family of Britain

© 2013

Mary Stuart, one of the most beautiful women of her times, was brought up in France and married the heir to the throne, an unattractive and sickly youth. Widowed at 18, she returned to Scotland and soon married her handsome but violent and dissolute cousin Henry, Lord Darnley, later strangled in Edinburgh. Mary then married the chief suspect, James Hepburn, the Earl of Bothwell. The outraged Scots forced her to flee to England; Bothwell deserted Mary, fled to Europe, and died mad in terrible conditions in a Danish prison. Mary was a very great threat to her cousin Queen Elizabeth I for nearly 20 years and was beheaded in 1587 after conspiring to have her murdered. Elizabeth's nearest male relative, and ultimately her heir, was James Stuart, son of Mary Queen of Scots and Darnley.

Descent of Queen Elizabeth II from King William I (the Conqueror)

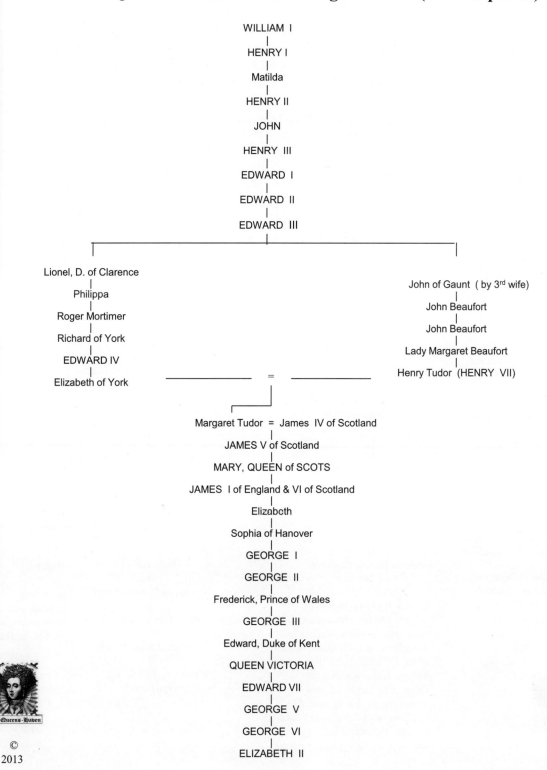

WILLIAM I
|
HENRY I
|
Matilda
|
HENRY II
|
JOHN
|
HENRY III
|
EDWARD I
|
EDWARD II
|
EDWARD III

Lionel, D. of Clarence
|
Philippa
|
Roger Mortimer
|
Richard of York
|
EDWARD IV
|
Elizabeth of York

John of Gaunt (by 3rd wife)
|
John Beaufort
|
John Beaufort
|
Lady Margaret Beaufort
|
Henry Tudor (HENRY VII)

——————— = ———————

Margaret Tudor = James IV of Scotland
|
JAMES V of Scotland
|
MARY, QUEEN of SCOTS
|
JAMES I of England & VI of Scotland
|
Elizabeth
|
Sophia of Hanover
|
GEORGE I
|
GEORGE II
|
Frederick, Prince of Wales
|
GEORGE III
|
Edward, Duke of Kent
|
QUEEN VICTORIA
|
EDWARD VII
|
GEORGE V
|
GEORGE VI
|
ELIZABETH II

©
2013

The Descent of Diana, Princess of Wales, from King Charles II

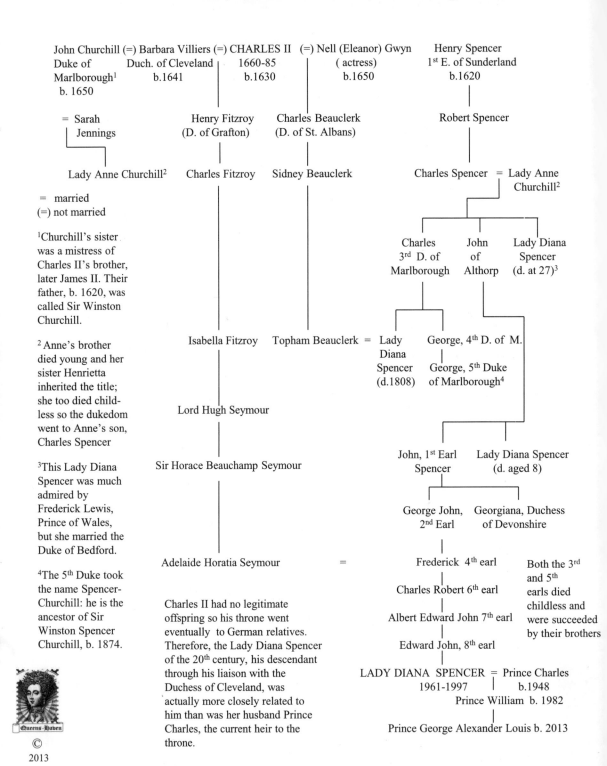

John Churchill (=) Barbara Villiers (=) CHARLES II (=) Nell (Eleanor) Gwyn   Henry Spencer
Duke of   Duch. of Cleveland   1660-85   (actress)   1st E. of Sunderland
Marlborough[1]   b.1641   b.1630   b.1650   b.1620
b. 1650

= Sarah   Henry Fitzroy   Charles Beauclerk   Robert Spencer
  Jennings   (D. of Grafton)   (D. of St. Albans)

Lady Anne Churchill[2]   Charles Fitzroy   Sidney Beauclerk   Charles Spencer = Lady Anne
                                                                                      Churchill[2]

= married
(=) not married

[1]Churchill's sister was a mistress of Charles II's brother, later James II. Their father, b. 1620, was called Sir Winston Churchill.

[2] Anne's brother died young and her sister Henrietta inherited the title; she too died childless so the dukedom went to Anne's son, Charles Spencer

[3]This Lady Diana Spencer was much admired by Frederick Lewis, Prince of Wales, but she married the Duke of Bedford.

[4]The 5th Duke took the name Spencer-Churchill: he is the ancestor of Sir Winston Spencer Churchill, b. 1874.

Charles   John   Lady Diana
3rd D. of   of   Spencer
Marlborough   Althorp   (d. at 27)[3]

Isabella Fitzroy   Topham Beauclerk = Lady   George, 4th D. of M.
                                       Diana
                                       Spencer   George, 5th Duke
                                       (d.1808) of Marlborough[4]

Lord Hugh Seymour

                                       John, 1st Earl   Lady Diana Spencer
                                       Spencer   (d. aged 8)

Sir Horace Beauchamp Seymour

                                       George John,   Georgiana, Duchess
                                       2nd Earl   of Devonshire

Adelaide Horatia Seymour   =   Frederick 4th earl   Both the 3rd
                                                                 and 5th
                                       Charles Robert 6th earl   earls died
                                                                 childless and
Charles II had no legitimate   Albert Edward John 7th earl   were succeeded
offspring so his throne went   by their brothers
eventually to German relatives.   Edward John, 8th earl
Therefore, the Lady Diana Spencer
of the 20th century, his descendant   LADY DIANA SPENCER = Prince Charles
through his liaison with the   1961-1997   b.1948
Duchess of Cleveland, was   Prince William b. 1982
actually more closely related to
him than was her husband Prince   Prince George Alexander Louis b. 2013
Charles, the current heir to the
throne.

© 2013

The Common Descent of Prince Charles and the Late Diana, Princess of Wales from Bess of Hardwick (c.1527 – 1608)

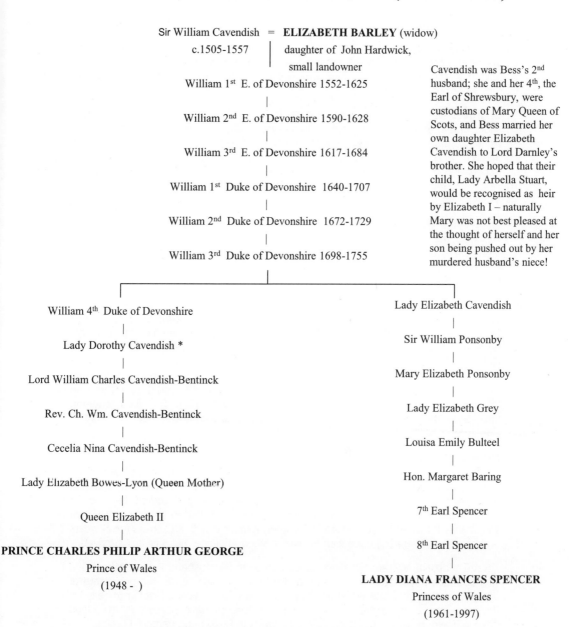

Sir William Cavendish = **ELIZABETH BARLEY** (widow)
c.1505-1557   daughter of John Hardwick,
small landowner

William 1st E. of Devonshire 1552-1625

William 2nd E. of Devonshire 1590-1628

William 3rd E. of Devonshire 1617-1684

William 1st Duke of Devonshire 1640-1707

William 2nd Duke of Devonshire 1672-1729

William 3rd Duke of Devonshire 1698-1755

Cavendish was Bess's 2nd husband; she and her 4th, the Earl of Shrewsbury, were custodians of Mary Queen of Scots, and Bess married her own daughter Elizabeth Cavendish to Lord Darnley's brother. She hoped that their child, Lady Arbella Stuart, would be recognised as heir by Elizabeth I – naturally Mary was not best pleased at the thought of herself and her son being pushed out by her murdered husband's niece!

William 4th Duke of Devonshire

Lady Dorothy Cavendish *

Lord William Charles Cavendish-Bentinck

Rev. Ch. Wm. Cavendish-Bentinck

Cecelia Nina Cavendish-Bentinck

Lady Elizabeth Bowes-Lyon (Queen Mother)

Queen Elizabeth II

PRINCE CHARLES PHILIP ARTHUR GEORGE
Prince of Wales
(1948 -)

Lady Elizabeth Cavendish

Sir William Ponsonby

Mary Elizabeth Ponsonby

Lady Elizabeth Grey

Louisa Emily Bulteel

Hon. Margaret Baring

7th Earl Spencer

8th Earl Spencer

LADY DIANA FRANCES SPENCER
Princess of Wales
(1961-1997)

* Lady Dorothy's brother, the 5th Duke of Devonshire, married the outrageous Georgiana Spencer (1757-1806), daughter of the first Earl Spencer; she sold kisses for votes for Charles James Fox in the 1784 General Election. Georgiana was a famous hostess, fashion icon and socialite who experimented with drugs and lost a fortune gambling. For years she lived in a ménage à trois with her husband and his mistress Bess Foster, who was also her best friend – the two friends were even expecting the duke's babies at the same time!

©
2013

The House of Hanover 1704-1910

Who Were They?

They were relatively minor German princes descended from James I through his daughter Elizabeth and there were nearly sixty possible candidates more closely related to the British Stuarts than was George I, but they were ineligible because they were not Protestants.

George I was not very inspiring, nor particularly bright, and understood very little about Britain and her people, which did him no credit, since he had known for years what his future had in store. He was further disadvantaged by being able to speak hardly a word of English, a shortcoming that led to the First Lord of the Treasury, Robert Walpole, having to preside over Cabinet meetings for him, thus becoming his First – or Prime – Minister. George had mistresses, but when his estranged wife took a lover it was common knowledge that her husband had him murdered.

The reign of **George II** saw the real beginning of Britain as a world power, and he was also the last monarch to lead an army into battle, in 1743 at Dettingen in Bavaria. He had many mistresses, whom his wife accepted with such good grace that he said not one of them was fit to buckle her shoe. The king and queen so detested their son **Frederick Lewis, Prince of Wales** that at his death they were said to have rejoiced at the thought of never seeing him again.

The first Hanoverian monarch born and bred in Britain was **George III**, a hard-working and caring man possibly afflicted by the blood disease porphyria, in his times diagnosed as madness. It was rumoured that George was married to Hannah Lightfoot, the daughter of a shoemaker from Wapping, and was the father of her 3 children; if this is so then the 15 children of his second, and therefore bigamous, marriage to **Queen Charlotte**, were not eligible to succeed to the throne, throwing the position of the current royal family open to speculation. The documentation believed by many at the time to be the genuine marriage certificate bearing George's signature, is held in the Royal Archive at Windsor.

George IV acted as Prince Regent in his father's last and long illness, but his legendary extravagance and dissolute lifestyle made him a cartoonists' dream by offering them an endless source of colourful subject-matter. Conveniently ignoring his own record, he put his wife on trial for adultery and locked her out of Westminster Abbey at his coronation. His only daughter died in childbirth. **William IV**, already 64 when he succeeded his brother, had lived with an actress for 22 years and had 10 children, but none with his wife, Queen Adelaide, half his age, survived.

Queen Victoria, William IV's niece, was devoted to her husband **Prince Albert** and was so much devastated by his early death from typhoid, due to the poor state of the royal drains, that she withdrew from public life for 13 years, leading to calls for the monarchy to be abolished. Victoria is believed to have passed on the blood disease haemophilia to later generations of royals in Russia and parts of Europe.

Edward VII became king at 59; despite having an attractive wife, he had a series of mistresses, but **Queen Alexandra** was comforted by the fact that, 'He always loved me best'. Even so, three of his favourites – Lily Langtry (*the Jersey Lily*), Frances Brooke, Countess of Warwick (*Darling Daisy*) and Mrs. Keppel, were invited to his coronation; Alice Keppel was the great-grandmother of Camilla Parker-Bowles.

The Hanoverians 1714 – 1910

(According to Salic law a woman could not reign in Hanover, so William IV was the last ruler of both Hanover & Britain)

GEORGE I = Sophia Dorothea
1660-1727 | of Brunswick-Celle

GEORGE II = Caroline of
1683 -1760 | Brandenburg-Ansbach

Frederick Lewis = Augusta   William   others
Prince of Wales | of Saxe-Gotha   Duke of Cumberland
1707-1751

GEORGE III = Charlotte of   others
1738-1820 | Mecklenburg-Strelitz

GEORGE IV = Caroline of	Frederick	WILLIAM IV = Adelaide of	Edward = Victoria of	Ernest	others
(Pr. Regent)	Brunswick	D. of York	1765-1837	Saxe-Meiningen	D. of Kent	Saxe-Coburg-	Augustus
1762-1830		d. 1827			1767-1820	Saalfeld	K. of Hanover

Princess Charlotte of Wales   (Alexandrina) VICTORIA = Albert of
1796-1817   1819-1901   Saxe-Coburg-Gotha

Her mother was his father's sister

Victoria, = Frederick III	EDWARD VII = Alexandra	Alice	Alfred	Helena	Louise	Arthur	Leopold	Beatrice
Princess	of Germany	(Albert Edward)	of Denmark		Duke of			Duke of	Duke of	
Royal		1841-1910			Edinburgh			Connaught	Albany	

Alix
(Tsarina Alexandra of Russia
murdered with all her family in 1918)

Victoria = Alfonso XIII
Eugenie | of Spain
(*Ena*)

Wilhelm II	Albert Victor (*Eddy*)	GEORGE V	Louise	Victoria	Maud = Haakon VII	Juan
Emperor of	Duke of	1865-1936			of Norway	
Germany	Clarence					King Juan Carlos
1859-1941	1864-1892					b.1938

My dear first-born is the greatest ass and the greatest liar and the greatest beast in the whole world,
and I heartily wish he were out of it.
Queen Caroline, consort of George II, on the subject of their own son Frederick Lewis, Prince of Wales.

©
2013

The House of Windsor 1917–
(1910 – 1917 the House of Saxe-Coburg and Gotha)

Who Are They?

They are the Hanoverians under another name. George V kept his grandfather Prince Albert's family name of Saxe-Coburg-Gotha until 1917, but the British animosity towards all things German as a result of the First World War made it expedient to change to something that sounded completely English – like *Windsor.* In many ways this was a big step forward because the Court still had a strong German flavour right up to the 20th century, a situation reinforced by the heirs to the throne marrying their German relatives. Indeed, the only rulers for nearly 300 years not to do this were Edward VII, whose wife was a princess of Denmark, Edward VIII, who married an American – and had to abdicate in order to do so, and his brother George VI who married the daughter of the Earl of Strathmore – but he had not expected to become king anyway.

If anybody knew the meaning of the words 'royal duty' it was Princess May of Teck, later **Queen Mary** and wife of **George V**, for when her fiancé **Albert Victor (Eddy)** died, his brother George not only inherited his place in the succession – he inherited the candidate for the arranged marriage as well! (May, and the country at large, could have had a narrow escape: as future king material Eddy was not showing a lot of promise and was attracted to the more seamy side of London life, which has led to speculation that he was involved in the Jack the Ripper murders – although it would appear there is no foundation in the accusations.) Although undoubtedly he thought he was a good parent, George V treated his children to a military-style regime and they sometimes feared him. Photographs of the Prince of Wales (Edward VIII) and the Duke of York (George VI) reveal them to be very sad-looking little boys, and the latter had a severe nervous stammer for the rest of his life.

Edward VIII, later Duke of Windsor, was christened Edward Albert Christian George Andrew Patrick David and was known as David to his family. His father wanted to call him Edward in memory of Prince Eddy, but Queen Victoria, who was determined to have all future kings named Albert, reminded him that his late brother was in fact called Albert Victor! The story of Edward/David's life makes for interesting reading – he was small of stature but good-looking, charming, a very snappy dresser and women of all social classes all around the world swooned over him. Although he showed early promise and an interest in the common people, Edward turned into little more than a playboy and serial womaniser and, as he was still unmarried and childless as he approached 40 it must surely have occurred to his brother Albert, the Duke of York, that his own daughter, Princess Elizabeth, was likely to succeed. Edward's father died in 1936 and the new king wanted a twice-divorced American socialite, **Wallis Simpson**, for his queen. When this was forbidden he decided to abdicate, and may have seen his situation as simply exchanging places with his younger brother and continuing to lead the good life in England, but it was not to be.

George VI (Albert, or 'Bertie') was not of a robust constitution and was initially thought ill-suited to the role of king – especially on the eve of a world war – but he did his best to discharge his duty, and his being a family man made the monarchy popular. Because of his severe stammer, making speeches was a nightmare for him. The strain of his job, coupled with years of heavy smoking, killed him at the age of 56. His wife, the former **Lady Elizabeth Bowes-Lyon**, who was 51 when he died, was the first British consort or ruler to reach 100 years of age.

The House of Windsor 1910 –

After I am dead the boy will ruin himself in twelve months.
George V talking to Prime Minister Stanley Baldwin about the Prince of Wales (Edward VIII)

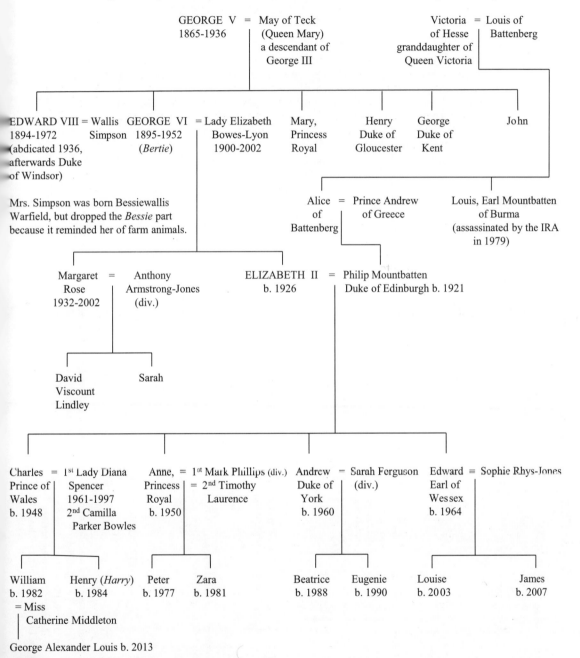

GEORGE V = May of Teck
1865-1936 (Queen Mary)
a descendant of
George III

Victoria = Louis of
of Hesse | Battenberg
granddaughter of
Queen Victoria

EDWARD VIII = Wallis   GEORGE VI = Lady Elizabeth   Mary,   Henry   George   John
1894-1972   Simpson   1895-1952   Bowes-Lyon   Princess   Duke of   Duke of
(abdicated 1936,   (*Bertie*)   1900-2002   Royal   Gloucester   Kent
afterwards Duke
of Windsor)

Mrs. Simpson was born Bessiewallis
Warfield, but dropped the *Bessie* part
because it reminded her of farm animals.

Alice = Prince Andrew   Louis, Earl Mountbatten
of | of Greece   of Burma
Battenberg   (assassinated by the IRA
in 1979)

Margaret = Anthony   ELIZABETH II = Philip Mountbatten
Rose   Armstrong-Jones   b. 1926   Duke of Edinburgh b. 1921
1932-2002   (div.)

David   Sarah
Viscount
Lindley

Charles = 1st Lady Diana   Anne, = 1st Mark Phillips (div.)   Andrew – Sarah Ferguson   Edward = Sophie Rhys-Jones
Prince of | Spencer   Princess | = 2nd Timothy   Duke of | (div.)   Earl of |
Wales   1961-1997   Royal   Laurence   York   Wessex
b. 1948   2nd Camilla   b. 1950   b. 1960   b. 1964
| Parker Bowles

William   Henry (*Harry*)   Peter   Zara   Beatrice   Eugenie   Louise   James
b. 1982   b. 1984   b. 1977   b. 1981   b. 1988   b. 1990   b. 2003   b. 2007
= Miss
| Catherine Middleton

George Alexander Louis b. 2013

A very pleasant middle to upper-class type of lady with a talkative retired Navy husband.
The journalist Malcolm Muggeridge on the subject of Queen Elizabeth II

Prince Philip of Greece and Denmark; Duke of Edinburgh, born 1921

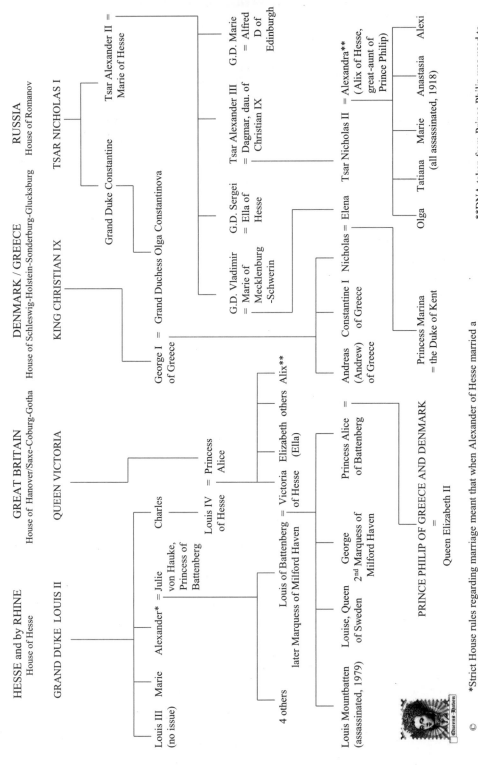

HESSE and by RHINE	GREAT BRITAIN	DENMARK / GREECE	RUSSIA
House of Hesse	House of Hanover/Saxe-Coburg-Gotha	House of Schleswig-Holstein-Sonderburg-Glucksburg	House of Romanov

GRAND DUKE LOUIS II   QUEEN VICTORIA   KING CHRISTIAN IX   TSAR NICHOLAS I

Tsar Alexander II = Marie of Hesse

Grand Duke Constantine

G.D. Marie = Alfred D of Edinburgh

Tsar Alexander III = Dagmar, dau. of Christian IX

George I = Grand Duchess Olga Constantinova
of Greece

G.D. Vladimir = Marie of Mecklenburg-Schwerin

G.D. Sergei = Ella of Hesse

Tsar Nicholas II = Alexandra** (Alix of Hesse, great-aunt of Prince Philip)

Marie   Alexander* = Julie von Hauke, Princess of Battenberg   Charles

Louis IV = Princess Alice of Hesse

Louis III (no issue)

Victoria = Louis of Battenberg later Marquess of Milford Haven   Elizabeth (Ella)   others   Alix**

of Hesse

Constantine I   Nicholas = Elena   Andreas (Andrew) of Greece = Princess Alice of Battenberg

Olga   Tatiana   Marie   Anastasia   Alexi
(all assassinated, 1918)

4 others

Louis Mountbatten (assassinated, 1979)   Louise, Queen of Sweden   George 2nd Marquess of Milford Haven

Princess Marina = the Duke of Kent

PRINCE PHILIP OF GREECE AND DENMARK
=
Queen Elizabeth II

© 2013

*Strict House rules regarding marriage meant that when Alexander of Hesse married a commoner he lost all rights to the throne for himself and his children and could not pass on his title. His wife was given the redundant title Princess of Battenberg so the children would inherit something, but they were to be the lower-status Serene, not Royal, Highnesses. In 1947 Prince Philip took his mother's anglicised name rather than the Schleswig-Holstein Sonderburg-Glucksburg of his father.

**DNA taken from Prince Philip was used to help identify the remains of his great-aunt, the last Tsarina of Russia.

23

Who Else Was Around?

Harold II (King of England)	1020-1066
El Cid (Rodrigo Diaz de Vivar)	1043-1099
Thomas Becket	1118-1170
Genghis Khan (Temu jan)	1162-1227
St. Francis of Assisi	1182-1226
Simon de Montfort	1208-1265
Marco Polo	1254-1324
Sir William Wallace	1270-1305
Geoffrey Chaucer	1340-1400
Joan of Arc	1412-1431
William Caxton	1422-1491
Botticelli (Sandro Filipepi)	1445-1510
Christopher Columbus	1451-1506
Leonardo da Vinci	1452-1519
Nicolaus Copernicus	1473-1543
Cardinal Wolsey	1473-1530
Michelangelo Buonarroti	1475-1564
Caesare Borgia	1476-1507
Sir Thomas More	1478-1535
Martin Luther	1483-1546
Thomas Cranmer	1489-1556
Hans Holbein (the younger)	1497-1543
(Michel) Nostrodamus	1503-1566
Ivan the Terrible	1530-1584
Sir Francis Drake	1540-1596
El Greco (D. Theotokopolos)	1541-1614
Sir Walter Raleigh	1554-1618
Galileo Galilei	1564-1642
Christopher Marlowe	1564-1593
William Shakespeare	1564-1616
Guy Fawkes	1570-1606
Sir Peter-Paul Rubens	1577-1640
Oliver Cromwell	1599-1658
Sir Anthony van Dyck	1599-1641
The Pilgrim Fathers	various
Rembrandt van Rijn	1606-1669
Sir Christopher Wren	1632-1723
Samuel Pepys	1633-1703
Louis XIV of France	1638-1715
Sir Isaac Newton	1642-1727
D. of Marlborough (Churchill)	1650-1722
Nell (Eleanor) Gwyn	1651-1687
Edmond Halley	1656-1742
George Fr. Handel	1685-1759
Johann Sebastian Bach	1685-1750
John Wesley	1703-1791
Benjamin Franklin	1706-1790
Capability (Lancelot) Brown	1715-1783
(Giovanni Giacomo) Casanova	1725-1788
Captain James Cook	1728-1779
Catherine the Great	1729-1796
George Washington	1732-1799
Edward Jenner	1749-1823
Marie Antoinette	1755-1793
Wolfgang Amadeus Mozart	1756-1791
William Blake	1757-1827
Lord (Horatio) Nelson	1758-1805
William Pitt, the Younger	1759-1806
Madame (Marie) Tussaud	1760-1850
D. of Wellington (Wellesley)	1769-1852
Napoleon Bonaparte	1769-1821
Ludwig van Beethoven	1770-1827
Jane Austen	1775-1817
Joseph M. W. Turner	1775-1851
Lord Byron (George Gordon)	1788-1824
Charles Darwin	1809-1882
Abraham Lincoln	1809-1865
Alfred, Lord Tennyson	1809-1892
Frédéric Chopin	1810-1849
Charles Dickens	1812-1870
David Livingstone	1813-1873
The Brontë Sisters	1818-1855
Karl Marx	1818-1883
Florence Nightingale	1820-1910
Louis Pasteur	1822-1875
The Tolpuddle Martyrs	various
Sitting Bull (Tatanka Iyotake)	1834-1890
General (George A.) Custer	1839-1876
Thomas Hardy	1840-1928
Claude Monet	1840-1926
Peter Illych Tchaikovsky	1840-1893
Vincent van Gogh	1853-1890
Oscar Wilde	1854-1900
Emmeline Pankhurst	1858-1928
Marie Curie	1867-1934
The Wright Brothers	1867-1948
Lenin (Vladimir Illych Ulyanov)	1870-1924
Rasputin (Grigori Efimovich)	1872-1916
Winston S. Churchill	1874-1965
Albert Einstein	1879-1955
Stalin (Josef V. Dzhugashvili)	1879-1953
Adolf Hitler	1889-1945

Monarchs Since 1066

Compiled from a wide variety of sources and checked against *Burke's Peerage, Complete Peerage,* information held in Brian Tompsett's *Royal Genealogical Database* at the University of Hull and *Britain's Royal Families – the Complete Genealogy*, by Alison Weir. Children include stillbirths, where known. (When voluminous gowns were in fashion, pregnancies could go almost unnoticed in some cases – so we may never know the full story.)

Monarch	Reigned	Cause of death	Died aged	Children born to spouse(s)	Children born to other(s)
William I	1066-1087	riding accident	59	10	?
William II	1087-1100	murdered	44	-	-
Henry I	1100-1135	food poisoning	67	4	17+1+3+1+1+2
Stephen	1135-1154	burst appendix?	57	5	3+2
Henry II[1]	1154-1189	fall from horse/fever	56	8	3+2+1+4
Richard I	1189-1199	wounds	42	-	-
John	1199-1216	overeating/ dysentery	49	5	1+1+10
Henry III	1216-1272	old age/stroke	65	9	-
Edward I	1272-1307	dysentery	68	16+3	-
Edward II	1207-1327	murdered	43	4	-
Edward III	1327-1377	dementia/stroke	64	13	4
Richard II	1377-1399	murdered	33	-	-
Henry IV	1399-1413	heart attack	46	7	-
Henry V	1413-1422	dysentery	34	1	-
Henry VI[2]	1422-1461	murdered	49	1	-
Edward IV	1461-1483	pneumonia?/ poison?	40	10	3
Edward V	1483	murdered	12	-	-
Richard III[3]	1483-1485	killed in battle	32	1	?
Henry VII	1485-1509	tuberculosis/ overwork	52	8	?
Henry VIII[4]	1509-1547	ulcerated leg/fever	55	7+3+1	1
Edward VI	1547-1553	tuberculosis	15	-	-
Mary I	1553-1558	cancer	42	-	-
Elizabeth I	1558-1603	pneumonia	69	-	-

[1] Henry II was a notorious womaniser whose best-known, and best-loved, mistress was Rosamund Clifford. Another, Ikeni, was referred to as a common prostitute, but may have been the daughter of a knight. Henry even had a liaison with his future daughter-in-law.

[2] Henry VI was a very chaste man who really believed that the Holy Spirit had visited his pregnant wife, but the less righteous thought it could have had been the Duke of Somerset!

[3] Alison Weir says that Richard III had 7 illegitimate offspring.

[4] Only 1 of Catherine of Aragon's babies survived (Mary I); Anne Boleyn had stillbirths and a miscarriage but her first child lived to become Queen Elizabeth I. Jane Seymour died shortly after the birth of her son, later Edward VI; all of Henry's last 3 wives failed to conceive. His only other known child is Henry Fitzroy, born to Elizabeth Blount.

James I	1603-1625	stroke	58	9	-
Charles I	1625-1649	beheaded	48	9	-
Commonwealth and Protectorate 1649-1660 (Oliver Cromwell)					
Charles II[5]	1660-1685	stroke	54	3 stillborn, 1 miscarriage	1+1+2+5+2+1 +1
James II	1685-1688 deposed	stroke	77	8+11	4+3
William III	1689-1702	fall from horse	51	3, all	-
& Mary II	1689-1694	smallpox	32	stillborn	-
Anne[6]	1702-1714	porphyria?	49	18	-
George I	1714-1727	stroke	67	2	2
George II	1727-1760	stroke	76	10	1?
George III[7]	1760-1820	porphyria?	81	15	3?
George IV[8]	1820-1830	stroke	67	1	1+1
William IV[9]	1830-1837	pneumonia	71	5	1+10
Victoria[10]	1837-1901	? natural causes	81	9	-
Edward VII	1901-1910	heart attack	68	6	-
George V	1910-1936	bronchitis/heart attack	70	6	-
Edward VIII	1936	cancer	77	-	-
George VI	1936-1952	cancer	56	2	-
Elizabeth II	1952-			4	-

[5] Charles II had a number of mistresses, including duchesses and actresses, one of the latter being Eleanor (Nell) Gwyn, who came from very humble beginnings. Nell and her great rival the Duchess of Portsmouth were known respectively as the Protestant and Catholic Whores.

[6] Queen Anne had 17 or 18 pregnancies. (Henry I holds the royal record so far with 29 children)

[7] Duty forced him to marry Charlotte of Mecklenberg-Strelitz, to whom he was a good husband, but there were rumours George III was already married to Hannah Lightfoot, the daughter of a Wapping shoemaker. He could have suffered from the blood disease porphyria, sometimes said, but not proven, to be the cause of questionable behaviour in later royals such as Prince Albert Victor (Eddy),

[8] George IV married Mrs. Maria Fitzherbert and was probably not divorced when he married Caroline of Brunswick, but this did not matter since the first marriage was not recognised in England because Mrs. Fitzherbert was a Roman Catholic. In the present-day Royal Family Prince Michael of Kent disqualified himself from the line of succession when he married Baroness Marie-Christine von Reibnitz (Princess Michael of Kent), a Roman Catholic.

[9] William IV, who as a younger son never expected to become king, lived a happy life with the actress Dorothea Jordan and their 10 children for 22 years until financial problems forced him to marry Princess Adelaide of Saxe-Meiningen, with whom he had no surviving children.

[10] Victoria's uncle, the odious Prince Regent, later George IV, caused chaos at her christening by refusing to let her have the name Georgiana Alexandrina Charlotte Augusta Victoria. He complained that his name could not be politely put before that of Tsar Alexander (one of the godfathers) so he would not allow its use at all. Charlotte was banned because it was the name of his late daughter. Whilst the Archbishop of Canterbury waited in disbelief, and the mother burst into tears, the Prince and the Duke of Kent, the baby's father, argued it out, eventually agreeing upon Alexandrina Victoria. Alexandrina, known as *Drina* until about the age of 9, preferred the name Victoria, her mother's name, and further attempts at changes failed.

Things They Said

I fear the anger I had recently shown against him may have been the cause of this misdeed (Becket's murder). I call God to witness that I am extremely disturbed, but more with my anxiety about my reputation than qualms of conscience.
Henry II writing to the Pope in 1171

My God! this is a wonderful land and a faithless one; for she has exiled, slain, destroyed and ruined so many kings, so many rulers, so many great men, and she is always diseased and suffering from differences, quarrels and hatred between her people.
Richard II's opinion as to the state of his kingdom, expressed whilst a prisoner in the Tower in 1399 – he was murdered at Pontefract Castle the following year

Everyone knows I act in everything with kindness and mercy, for I am forcing Rouen into submission by starvation, not by fire, sword or bloodshed.
Henry V, to a delegation from the city of Rouen, 1415

I never longed so much for a thing as I do to see you and to speak with you…it makes my heart die that I cannot always be in your company.
Queen Katherine Howard to Master Thomas Culpeper in the spring of 1541 – both were executed by her husband King Henry VIII

And therefore I am come amongst you as you see at this time not for my recreation and disport, but being resolved in the midst and heat of the battle to live or die amongst you all. To lay down for God and my kingdom and for my people my honour and my blood even in the dust. I know I have the body of a weak and feeble woman, but I have the heart and stomach of a King, and of a King of England too.
Queen Elizabeth I on the eve of the invasion of the Spanish Armada, 1588

I would rather have a plain russet-coated captain that knows what he fights for, and loves what he knows, than that which you call a gentleman and is nothing else.
Letter written by Oliver Cromwell, 1643

…a violator of his word, a libertine over head and ears in debt and disgrace…a man who has just closed half a century without one single claim on the gratitude of his country or the respect of posterity.
The writer/journalist Leigh Hunt describing the Prince Regent, later George IV, in 1812. Hunt was sent to prison for two years for this

…I stood up, kissing his dear heavenly forehead & called out in a bitter agonising cry: "Oh! My dear Darling!" & then dropped to my knees in a mute, distracted despair, unable to utter a word or shed a tear!
Queen Victoria's own account of her reaction to the death of Prince Albert, 1861